CACHE THE CZECH
Book II

Good King Wenceslaus
and
Others From Prague

Father Walter Marek

SMD Books
Traverse City, Michigan

Cache The Czech: Good King Wenceslaus

SMD Books
smdbooks@excite.com

Compiled & Edited: Deanna D. Siler
Cover Design: Deanna D. Siler

ISBN–13: 978-0-9798432-1-1
ISBN–10: 0-9798432-1-9

Printed by Signature Book Printing
www.sbpbooks.com

Contents

Contents

Acknowledgements

I wish to express my heartfelt gratitude to several people in the writing of this book. It is a compilation of my memories growing up in Prague and the saints, the people, the invasions, and the lessons learned from a very long life.

I am indebted to my caring friend, Mrs. Marie "Muggs" Richards, whose gentle urging and watchful eye has kept me from giving up on the idea of another book. She has cared for me during the writing of this book, kept me healthy, and has been an encouragement for me.

Midway through the writing of this book, there was a glitch with the original recorder. The transcript of the book came up missing. Through the persistence of my editor, Deanna and her husband, Bill, the missing pages were found and the book has been completed.

It is my belief that those who read this book will be delighted with the information herein. It's not every day we can find a historical recording of the events that changed the world forever written by someone who lived them. In my ninety-one years of life I have seen the tranquility of my country torn apart, invaded, and changed. In all of this there remained hope for a better future and the music that has been so prevalent in Prague.

Father Walter Marek
Traverse City, Michigan 2009

Introduction

Prague is considered one of the most beautiful cities in the world. In German, it is "Prag", in Spanish, it is "Praga", and in Czech, it is "Praha". It is uncertain how this name developed. It seems that the word "Praha" is from a Czech word, "Prah", which means threshold. The ancient business people were always amazed by the location, especially the Arabs and the other merchants from the East. They called it "threshold of heaven". In the opera of Bedrich Smetana, "Libuse", who was the first Duchess of Bohemia, sings, "I see a big city, the glory of which will reach the heavens." In the prehistoric times, "Libuse" was the Duchess of Bohemia. When she was selected, some man said, "Whoa to the men who are governed by the woman." Libuse selected her husband, Premysl, who was the forefather of many great Bohemian kings, dukes and princes for several centuries, called "premyslovci".

Good King Wenceslas

John Mason Neale — English

Chapter 1

Saint Wenceslaus

Good King Wenceslaus is known in America as the subject of a Christmas carol. He was a Duke of Bohemia, not a king. Bohemia is part of the present Czech Republic, with Moravia and part of Silecia. In German, Wenceslaus is "Wenzel" or "Wendel", and in the Czech language, "VACLAV". Bohemia was always a country important to Europe. As the chancellor of Prussia, Bismarck, once said, "He who dominates Bohemia dominates Europe."

After the death of his father, Vratislav I, Duke of Bohemia from the Premysl dynasty, when Saint Wenceslaus was 13 years old, he was brought up by his grandmother, Saint Ludmila, who was the first Czech princess. With her husband, Borivoj, they were the first Czechs baptized by Saints Cyril and Methodius, the "apostles to the Slavs". Ludmila raised Wenceslaus as a Christian, and was such a great influence on her grandson, that his mother, Drahamira, who was the daughter of a pagan tribal chief of Havolans, hated Ludmila. She was so furious about losing influence over her son, that she arranged to have Ludmila strangled. Ludmila became the first Czech Saint after she was murdered.

Saint Wenceslaus became the Duke of Bohemia at a very young age, about 18. He was above all kings and emperors of the day, because, while they couldn't read or write, Saint Wenceslaus was educated in Regensburg, and he could speak Latin, Greek, German and Czech.

Regensburg, in Bavaria at that time, was a very powerful country, and politically, Bohemia was their interest. Saint Wenceslaus had a challenge when the Bavarian army entered Bohemia. He faced the army, confronted the leader, and told him, "Let us not waste the blood of our people. Let us talk." He negotiated peace and promised to pay a yearly obligation of a hundred bulls. He knew that if his army lost, there would be much more pain and suffering.

Wenceslaus continued reigning in his land in charity and peace. He was usually accompanied by his servant, Podivin, when he was doing charity work. Podivin was always cold in winter, and Saint Wenceslaus told him, "Step in my footsteps, and you will be warm." That was the first of many miracles that would happen. The country was divided, from then until now, between Catholics and non-Catholics. Saint Wenceslaus had problems with the rebellious noble men, who did not want to be ruled by the Duke of Prague. One of them, "VRACLAV", who was from Eastern Bohemia, and who had the castle in the village of VRACLAV, not too far from the place called Horni Jeleni, which is where The Czech Music Camp for Youth is today. He gathered some little army and challenged Saint Wenceslaus. Both armies faced each other, and then St. Wenceslaus said to VRACLAV, "Let us not shed the blood of these innocent people." Let us decide who will be the Duke of Bohemia. VRACLAV started to move on Saint Wenceslaus, when suddenly, he saw two Angels behind St. Wenceslaus, protecting him. He got off his horse, knelt down, and pledged allegiance to St. Wenceslaus. He attended mass everyday and continued in charity, helpful to people.

There was a plot to get rid of Saint Wenceslaus when his brother, Boleslav, invited him to his castle, about 40 minutes north of Prague. When he went to mass that morning, he was attacked by a group of men which included his brother, Boleslav. He was able to escape, and ran to the church, but the door was locked. He couldn't open it. There, at the door, he was caught by his brother, where his brother killed him. "God forgive you for this, brother.", he said as he uttered his last words. Later, they transferred his body to Prague, and he is now buried in a special chapel called St. Wenceslaus Chapel. It is decorated with semi-precious stones.

When 1000 years passed, in 1929, a jubilee was celebrated. I was a student in Prague then. Composer Bohuslav Foester composed a great cantata for the occasion. Part of it was a children's choir to which Ladialav Sirovy and I were chosen from our school. He had a beautiful alto voice, and went on to become the Father at Notre Dame / Holy Cross and became the Master of the order, Holy Cross Fathers. It was a great opportunity for an eleven year old boy to be able to learn from all the professional singers and conductors, so I was very observant. There were 35 of us from Prague. We received a nice Saint Wenceslaus golden medallion for the honor. Here is the hymn we sang, which for a millennium, kept the faith of Saint Wenceslaus alive.

Hymn to St. Wenceslaus / Hymn to Sv Vaclav

Holy Wenceslaus, Duke of Bohemia
Pray for us
Pray for us to God,
To the Holy Spirit
Christe Eleison
You inherited Bohemia, Moravia, and Silecia
Do not let us die out
Us and our children,
Holy Wenceslaus

5

Chapter 2

Saints Cyril and Methodius

In the 9th Century, Emperor Svatopluk of Moravia, asked the Emperor in Istanbul to send some missionaries to our Czech country. The emperor selected two brothers from Salonica who were monks and knew the Slavic language because they lived near Bulgaria. They prepared themselves for missionary work and devised the Slavic alphabet from the Greek one. They translated some parts of the Bible to the old Slavic language. At that time, there was one Slavic language for all Slavic nations. They came on foot to the country, and were lodged in Velehrad. From Velehrad, they made it on foot to Prague. There was a very interesting road called Trstenice Road. That road was marked in history by religious monuments. Trstenice was a little village where I was an administrator from Litomysl. Today, no one can find those monuments. It is called Trstenice because around Litomysl flows a river which used to be called Trstenice, but is called Loucna now. It was very beautiful to find some traces of that special road taken by Saints Cyril and Methodius from Moravia to Bohemia. There, they baptized the grandparents of Saint Wenceslaus: Borivoj, and his wife, Ludmila. Because they could speak to the people and explain the Bible, they were very successful. However, the religious officers in Regensburg insisted that Bohemia, Moravia and Silecia were their interests, and they hated

Saints Cyril and Methodius. They accused them in Rome of taking away territory that was theirs and both had to go on foot to Rome to explain their situation.

In Rome, they successfully explained and defended their position. Cyril died there in Rome, and his brother, Methodius, was made Archbishop of this new territory. He came back to the Czech Republic to continue his work. However, the bishops in the surrounding territories didn't like it. They constantly talked about him to Rome, but the Holy Father at that time protected him. One Archbishop went so far as to put him in jail at one point. Eventually, the western liturgy of the church prevailed. Today, we have the Byzantine Liturgy as historical fact, and we have one hymn that Methodius taught his people. He taught the people to sing.

It always finished with the Greek: kyrie eleison, "Lord, have mercy" The Czech people didn't like that , so they made their own words, "Krles". This hymn was sung after the devotion on Sundays. The cathedral had four outstanding voices hired from retired opera singers. I remember Basso, when he sang the "krles". His sound was so wonderful, you could hear it over all the huge organ pipes, some up to sixty feet long.

Lord God love us, love us (4x)

Lord God love us and save us (4x)

Chapter 3

Charles IV, Holy Roman Emperor

The Czech King became the Holy Roman Emperor in the 14th century, from 1346 – 1376. His name was Charles the Fourth. His birth name was Wenceslaus (Vaclav), named after his maternal grandfather. His parents were John and Elisabeth I of Bohemia in Prague. He spent 7 years with his uncle, Charles IV of France, during which time he chose the name Charles at his confirmation. I have not found his name in any English History books. I wonder why? Maybe it is because he never went to war.

During his reign, Europe was completely peaceful, and cathedrals and universities were built. He was a man who understood the century. Charles IV is known by the bridge in Prague that he built, the Charles Bridge. He also built a wall for people who were hungry during a terrible famine. He gave poor people food in exchange for work to build the wall, which is now known as the "Hunger Wall". He was a man of honor who admired St. Wenceslaus, a patron saint and martyr, very much.

Charles IV was married 4 times. He had 2 daughters, Margaret and Catherine, by his first wife, Blanche, (1316 – 1348). His second marriage to Anna of Bavaria, (1329 – 1353), produced one son, Wenceslas, who died young. His third wife, Anna von Schweidnitz (1339 – 1362), had two children, Wenceslaus and Elizabeth. Wenceslaus was Charles' successor to the throne as Emperor and King of Bohemia. His fourth wife, Elizabeth of Pomerania, (1345 or 1347 – 1393), bore 6 children: Anne, Sigismund, John, Charles, Margaret, and Henry.

Charles was a very religious man. Every year, during Lent, he stopped doing everything and went to Karlstein Castle, which was named after him. There, he lived in the Chapel of The Holy Cross, where he prayed, meditated, and enjoyed the solitude. When he came home, he was ready to deal with the many things he had to face.

He started the first university in central Europe, in Prague, Charles University. Through his influence, Prague was given its first Archbishop of Prague, Arnost from Pardubice (a city in East Bohemia). He became the first chancellor of the university.

Charles was also a devotee to relics. In his day, it was customary for the Christians to have some relics of the saints. Unfortunately, it developed into a business where they preyed on poor people to sell them relics that weren't genuine. As students, we would laugh about it. I remember one instance where someone was trying to sell a feather from the wing of Archangel Gabriel.

Charles studied in Paris. His teacher was a cardinal who later became the pope. From Paris, he brought grape roots into the country and started vineyards, which are still prospering today.

Chapter 4

St. Adalbert

In Czech, St. Adalbert is "Vojtech", and in Polish, it is "Wojciech". He was the Czech who became the second bishop of Prague. It was a great honor that our own priest became our bishop. St. Adalbert cared very much about happenings in his country and noticed a lot of paganism. He believed in honoring God, while many of his people, including nobility, practiced paganism. The frustration was so great for him, that he left the country and went to Rome. The Czechs called him back and promised that they would do better. When he came back to the country, he heard that his family had all been killed. He didn't stay, and continued on his journey to Poland. Unfortunately, in Poland, he and his companions stepped on some pagan holy ground. The people caught him and murdered him. The question now is whether his body is in Poland or in Prague. Both claim to have his body. He is the patron Saint of the Czech and Polish nation.

When we celebrated the 600th anniversary of his death, it was about 1947. We celebrated in a special way. In Prague, they had a skull, and a special car, in which the skull of St. Adalbert was placed, so that the car went throughout the country and people could venerate St. Adalbert. When the car with St. Adalbert's skull came to Litomysl, I organized a great procession. At least 10,000 people came to see the skull of St. Adalbert and honor him as a martyr and patron of our country.

Chapter 5

St. John Nepomicene

Nepomicene means "from Nepomuk". He was a priest who was the Archbishop's right hand man, a very influential man in the archdiocese of Prague. The king was very jealous of his wife. He called St. John to ask him what she confessed to him. Naturally, he refused to say anything, and the king, in his anger, killed him. He ordered St. John Nepomicene to be thrown from the Charles Bridge into the river, and drowned. This was not the end, however, because, like a miracle, several bright stars appeared where the body was drowned. The people then went and recovered the body. He was buried as a saint and martyr. Many European rivers pay tribute to St. John Nepomicene. His statue can be seen all over Europe on various bridges, because he was thrown from a bridge. Every year, on his feast day, May 15th, there is a big procession in Prague honoring St. John. As a student, I always participated in it. We headed up the steep streets and headed past the institution for blind people, where their band always played for us as we marched by. Then we reached the cathedral, where he is buried in a silver coffin, made totally of silver. His tongue was given special honor because he never revealed anything from confessions. Today, his tongue is still preserved in a special reliquiary by his coffin.

Chapter 6

My Three Friends in Praque

You meet such friends only once in a lifetime. The first was Dr. La dislav Vachulka, professor of music and virtuoso on organ. He was my teacher at the gymnasium school and later in life, we became friends. About 3 years ago, I was celebrating a Mass at St. Adalbert-Vojtech in Praque, where Antonin Dvo rak, was the organist, and he designed this organ himself. The organist, who played very well, came down from the choir with great difficulty, because she was handicapped. I talked to her and asked her where she studied the organ. To my surprise, she replied "With Professor Dr. Ladislv-Vachlka." The church was attended by older people, who sang a very beautiful hymn to the Blessed Mother, which I did not know. The ending was, "We honor you and we love you, from our whole heart, Maria."

The second friend was a polyhistorian, Dr. Vaclav Wagner, who was the President of the International Club and Chairman of the office for Antiquities in Praque, for the whole Republic of Czechoslovakia. A polyhistorian is a person who knows everything that is known at that time. His knowledge was about arts, math, astronomy, and music. He knew all the Ambassadors in Prague, the President and the Secretaries of State. He was in contact with me, when I was hiding, and negotiated for me the contacts and the final escape in 1949.

The third special friend in Prague was Dr. Ladislav Pinkas. We met because of the second friend. He was a lawyer at the British Embassy in Prague. He accompanied me to the American Embassy, where I had an appointment with the military attache' Nowak.

Dr. Pinkas immigrated to England and made it to the United States. The family of American Ambassador Steinhart let him use a cottage on the St. Mary River in Maryland. The cottage was not modernized and had no heat or other conveniences. He was there completely alone and unhappy. He wrote me letters, which broke my heart, because I was unable to help him. I was only an assistant priest in the parishes with no power of decision. He wanted to teach for the State University in East Lansing, Michigan and I had no possibility at that time to help him. Finally, he went back to England, sick and old. He died in a home run by Christian Brothers. They let me know that he died, completely left alone and desolate. His sister Ms. Anne Pinkas was well known in Prague because she was secretary to the Chinese Ambassador. She was secretly taken to Paris by the French Military attache', who became persona non grata by Foche', the Czech communists. He left Prague after many years of serving and loving the country. Mrs. Pinkas lived in Paris and sent me several letters in the United States. When she died, the family ended with her.

Chapter 7

John Hus

Prague had a very good preacher in the 15th century. His name was John Hus. He was fed up with the irregularities and shenanigans in the Catholic Church. His preaching on Indulgences caused a lot of stir among the people. Eventually, he was called to the church council in Constance. He was supposed to explain and defend his teachings. He could not do it well. He was given over to the authorities of the Roman Empire and immediately burned at the stake. That was a very unfortunate move which stirred many Czechs. They organized in the form of an army of Hussites. This became a very powerful army which threatened all of Europe. Their methods were cruel and swift. Whenever they conquered a city, they destroyed the monasteries and killed all the monks on their pitchforks. They took a monk and threw him in the air and put him on several pitchforks and threw him in the fire. Fortunately, they never conquered Prague and two other big Catholic cities. They conquered Litomysl, the place where I lived for seven years. They destroyed the bishop's place and everything else so that the city never recovered. The Catholic side, as they called it, had an army too and finally defeated the Hussites who were at the end of their power anyway and were disorganized. After that, peace never came to our country. Even today, we are a divided people between the Catholics and the other Hussites. When I went to public grade school in Horni Jeleni, the school, teachers and about half the population were Hussites. My father suffered because he was one of the leaders in the church and in the political party which was called the Popular Party. For instance, in 1925 my Dad went to Rome for a pilgrimage. That created a great uproar and when he came back he was ridiculed in the newspaper which said on the first page, "Marek kisses the Pope's slippers" and after that was the article about his stay in Rome. Shortly after that, in the garden that we had behind the city, the Hussites stole all the young trees, and they put a message on the gate, "Mr. Marek, go ask the Pope who stole it?" In our town things were quite bad. I heard in one instance that some teachers gave bad marks to a student who was in the church on Sunday.

One incident stays in my memory today. It was about 1921 when the Catholic gymnists organization called the Eagles had a big regional conference in East Bohemia. On Sunday the Eagles had a parade through town. They did not know however, that the Hussites were waiting to beat them. The procession had about 1,000 or more people consisting of children, teens and adults. The men were always the last in the procession. The group of Hussites were hiding on a side street waiting for this procession – several thousands of them. They were armed with clubs and brass knuckles. They let the children and women pass. When the men appeared the Hussites came out with a big red flag with a big chalice on it . This was a symbol of anti-Catholicism. They attacked the men. The men were completely surprised. The leader of the Eagles told them to STOP ! Near by there was a big picket fence. He ordered all to take a picket out and use it for defense. My dad had a scar on his hand where someone tried to hit him with a stick. The eagles put up a great fight defending themselves, therefore, the Hussities concentrated on a man who held the big flag and tried to steal it. It would be a great victory for them. The flag man resisted but was overpowered. When this was seen by a priest from our parish who was a great man, a giant like, he took the flag into his hands from the flagman. Unfortunately, someone hit him on the head from the back. He lost consciousness and fell to the ground. He held tight to the flag even though they tried to get it from him. There ended the fight.

Chapter 8

Swedes in Prague

The whole of Europe was divided into two sides, Protestants and Catholics. It was said at the time that "cuius region illus religio" (if the head man was a certain religion all the people have to follow), that started the thirty year war from 1618 to 1648.

The Protestant part was mainly financed by Gustav the King of Sweden and the Catholic part by Austri and the Pope. I remember in grade school the teacher was delighted he could tell us about a Cardinal, who on the Catholic side was dressed in regalia, ran away and lost his hat when the Catholics were losing. The Protestants kept it and thought it a great prize and they still show this hat in the museum. During this time the persecution of Catholics was prevalent.

The Thirty Years War ended on Charles Bridge. The Swedish Army was trying to get across the bridge, but there was a group of about 200 students led by Father Plachy. The Swedes were stopped and left Prague, but they took all they could by stealing and robbing every business and household. They also stole a special hand Bible called Codes Argenteous. They took it and placed it in Upsala at the University. I wanted to see it so I took a train from Stockholm on Saturday. When I got there the library was closed. I stopped a professor and asked if I could see it. He let me in and left me alone. They also had in their library writings written by St. Bridgette. On Sunday, I went to Mass in Stockholm, which was to honor St. Bridgette. The choir at the Mass was a group of Protestant students who volunteered to sing for the special occasion. Afterwards, I met the conductor. He had been in Michigan once before so we had a good conversation.

The Swedish people were involved in European politics. In the last war, I was able to buy a nice Swedish washing machine and my dad bought lots of Swedish steel, which was the best of all. He invested money into a little tool shop. They would make the steel into tools.

Chapter 9

The Germans in Prague

German people always lived in our country. They lived separately and kept their language. It used to be said the best German language was heard in Prague. Some of them lived their whole life in Prague and never learned the Czech language. Even the writer Kafka wrote all his writings in German. I once met a German lady at the Blue Lake Fine Arts camp, who lived her whole life in Prague but was forced to leave at the end of the war, when the Germans were allowed to leave. She also didn't learn the Czech language.

There are two universities in Prague, Czech and German. Unfortunately, the symbols and banners, which were the Czech University were stored in the German University. There was a great fight for it, led by law student, Zeinger. He was from our Catholic school and later I met him in Germany as a refugee. The fights were daily for the banners. The police were not allowed to enter the university so they could not intervene. When Hitler came to power he wanted the Germans in all the countries to become a fifth wheel, an expression which means they wanted to be part of the Great Germany. The story of the Germans on Sudeten Land in the Czech Republic was told many times. They wanted to be brought to Germany. After the war, which was a loss for Germans , our president proclaimed, "If Germany you want, to Germany you will go." About 3 million of them went. It was a very unfortunate movement which created so much suffering and tears. Imagine a small city of 5000 to leave everything as it is and go by foot to Germany with only 2 pieces of luggage. I remember one village had a priest with them. On the way 80 older people died and he took care of them. It was a great chaos, and my pastor and I tried to help our 10 German parishes. In the Vicariate, they were all rich parishes, lots of fields and land. My pastor made it possible that all the 10 priests did not have to leave immediately, but they could hire a truck and load it with everything they owned and go to Austria. I had to congregate them all in one parish, it was a very bad time for me to see all the old priests be taken out of their parishes and brought to our Czech parish and wait for the trucks to arrive. They all made it to Austria.

During the war the Germans were on the top. When they started losing the war, the situation changed. For instance, Prague revolted against the Germans. It was a heroic act and no one knew how it would end. One Czech cut all the telephones of the Germans so they couldn't communicate. Still Germans were gaining because they had great numbers of SS people (like marines) in Prague.

Nobody knew or remembered the Russian soldiers who were stationed by Prague, they were called Vlasov. Vlasov was a Russian general who came to the Germans and offered them help. They organized about 200,000 soldiers, former POWs who were stationed all over Europe. They never helped because he was a drunk, and the Germans never trusted him. However, there was a group of 20,000 Vlasov soldiers that were asked to come to Prague and defeat the Germans. The Germans were able to negotiate a solution. They were given a way out to the north with all the soldiers and Germans. They were given a corridor north to Germany, all of them without harm. That left the Soviet army and American army only 25 miles from Prague at the time. It is said that the American army was prohibited by the Russians to help the Czechs. They wanted the city to fall and make us liberated, like in Warsaw, Poland and other cities. The Russians acted as conquerors. I was in Litomysl when the first Russian army came to town and they staged a beautiful celebration. There was one man in town that knew the Russians, the former prisoner of war from World War One. They had a beautiful band with them that played a concert, and a horse show. I was quite interested in the show and admired it. One man came up to me and said, " You should see what they do in the country". In Litomysl we didn't suffer because we had Russian partisans, who were friendly to us and we were friendly to them. It was a different situation completely. The Russian soldiers were told to be friendly to us. In other places they were known to steal lots of things, bikes, watches etc. "davaj hoginky" ("give me your watch") some soldiers had full arms of stolen watches.

Chapter 10

Kolakovsky Spy in Prague

Such conditions in the Russian army enabled one Catholic priest Yarof Kolakovsky. He became a super spy and pretended to be a Russian doctor and general. He went to the Russian headquarters in Poland and traveled freely with the military to Moscow. He was lodged in a place called Lubjanka. Lubjanka was one of the most infamous Russian prisons. It was also used as a dormitory for traveling people like him or for the wives of generals and others who were in the war. He described the conditions there in a book called God Is Underground. He found lots of faith in Russia and he describes how he handled the women who wanted him. He said to them, "...and how is your mother?". It always changed the girls; they started talking about their mother and changed the subject. I used the same question when I was a chaplain in the refugee camp and met some girls, who changed so much from the stay in the camp. I said, "How is your mother, do you hear from her?" They would tell me all about themselves and start to cry, the conversation would be completely different. Being away from their mothers was always very dangerous.

Otto Skorzeny was the greatest German spy. He was very daring. He put on the uniform of a United States officer because he spoke perfect English. He went to the headquarters of the American army and operated there. He also spoke Russian and did the same. He put on the uniform of the Russian officers and went to Moscow, the headquarters of the Russian army. He was favored by Hitler. He was also a leader of the German army and liberated Mussolini. I spoke to a lawyer here in Michigan after I came here. I spoke to a judge from Saginaw who was stationed after the war in Germany He told me that he, himself, had interrogated Skorzcny, but, he let him go because he couldn't find any crime he had committed. Skorzcny moved immediately from Germany to Portugal.

There were two English spies, Carlos and Phillby, who worked for Russia. They had come from England and found asylum in Prague. Carlos was the most interesting agent in the cold war. He was the most powerful. All the nations in Europe were afraid of him. Finally, he found the refugees in Prague in the Continental Hotel, living luxuriously. The Czech secret police went to talk to him to persuade him to leave, but, he stayed.

Chapter 11

The French in Prague

French and Czech people are almost always co-operating especially when, George Bedell was the Prime Minister of France. When the Communists took over our country, the French people did everything possible for us. For instance, they promised to help our leader, Monsignor Sramek, to escape. Everything was all set. The French airplane would come to a small airport outside of Prague and two leaders of our party, M. Sramek and M. Hala, both Catholic priests were going in a car on which the driver put a license plate which indicated that the car belonged to diplomats so they would never be stopped by the police. They safely got to the airport and waited for the plane there. The plane came on time, flew down, but the pilot noticed something funny. He saw some policemen in the woods waiting for them and took off right before landing. M. Sramek and M. Hala rushed towards the plane and into the hands of police. That didn't stop us from helping them from getting them out yet. They were arrested and taken to a castle high on the hill in Moravia. My two helpers, Smutek and my secretary, went to see if there was another place to land the plane. They came back telling me it was impossible. Later on, French military attaché General Foche, who loved Prague , was very friendly to the Pinkas family. He came to Prague and was stationed there many years. Ms. Ann Pinkas was the secretary to the Chinese ambassador in Prague. General Foche took her across the border with him thus she made it to Paris. There she promoted our Czech interests and wrote several letters about her brother, Liladslav Pinkas , who lived in the United States. She wrote me several letters.

French people in the Embassy of Prague always promised to take care of me. The situation worsened. They could not do much for me, so our underground took care of me.

Chapter 12

Jews in Prague

The Jews in Prague always lived in the ghetto. They were a minority until about the 19th century. They were much maligned by a street mob in Prague in times of some trouble. Whenever some sickness or problems appeared in Prague they would blame it on the Jews, "Let's go beat up the Jews." They ran into a 'Jewish town' and did all the damage they could to the Jews. This went on for many centuries until the Jews could have property and attend schools as others. During the Nazi occupation, Jews suffered completely. Very few came back after the Holocaust. The selection for Jewishness by Nazi's was very strict. I was one of the lucky ones. I was non-Arian. If you had one Jewish grandparent you were called non-Arian (like me) and if you had 2 Jewish grandparents you were Jewish. The code for this was very strict for Secret Service (SS) and Gestapo people. They had a special passport called, "ahnen pass," which meant, "passport of former family tree." Once, a high officer SS, came to our office in Litomysl. I was surprised, but he was actually nice. He asked me to look back in the church ancestry 200 years back. They had to fill out the passport 300 years back to verify that their ancestry was not Jewish, our records were complete from 1620 and on the first page of the record book said that the previous records were destroyed in a fire. Another time a lady came to our office, she was dressed well and was about 50 years old. She started crying and handed me her baptism record. "Look what you sent me, I can't show it to my husband he is a high government official." I copied the record as it was and it showed that her father was a comedian and circus act and this bothered her terribly. I had to change it somehow, it was very risky, but I had to do it. I omitted those words for her.

Prague had many outstanding Jewish people. I remember one very famous conductor George Zcell who for eighteen years conducted the German opera in Prague, and after that was the conductor for the Cleveland Orchestra. Under his baton the orchestra in Cleveland became the best in the world.

The Jewish doctors in Prague were some of the most skilled doctors. I remember one named Levi. He escaped Nazis before they came to our country and according to his wife, who was a singer, he worked during the war on a ship as a doctor. His wife told me they belonged to the free Masons. I asked her to tell me more about them. She told me that Masons in Prague was an organization for social purposes. They had as members people of money and influence and she said that sometimes after hours they would call the jazz band and they would come to the masons to play until 7 am in the morning as people danced. When Hitler came to Prague he closed all the lodges.

Chapter 13

Holy Infant of Prague

The devotion to Jesus as a little child spread very fast throughout the whole world, especially the Spanish speaking. In the United States, the Holy Infant of Prague has a beautiful statue in almost every Catholic home.

When my colleague Ludvik Nemec, immigrated to the Unites States, he published a book Holy Infant of Prague, in which he explained the origin and fast development of this devotion.

Unfortunately, over the years, the Czech people have forgotten the Holy Infant and no devotion developed in and by the Catholic Church. We were told that The Statue of the Holy Infant was in Prague and much sought by the tourists. During the time, when I was active in the Underground, I stopped at the church, where the statue was to pray. Next door were the offices of my friend, Dr. Vaclav Wagner, who offered me valuable advice. He was in contact with London during the war. At the end of the war, he was a member of the Committee which was in charge of the Prague upraising. There were about three members on the committee from the Communist Party. Those were strictly faithful to the Party and the orders from the Russians, who were only about 25 miles from Prague and offered no help.

When I was a Catholic Chaplain for the Refugees in Germany, I had a beautiful surprise. It was the gift from America, from the National Alliance of Czech Catholics. Among the different gifts were some booklets about the Holy Infant of Prague, with a beautiful song, which was unknown to me, but I liked it and taught it immediately to our children, forming a choir. The text was very timely for the refugees (Translated into English) "O, Holy Infant of Prague, you are our Divine Child. You can make our souls, which suffer, holy and mild." The song was written in two parts. When our children sang it in our simple chapel, all of us had tears in our eyes. We were all refugees, displaced persons, and our souls were all stricken by an unfulfilled desire for home.

Chapter 14

The Americans in Prague

The Americans are always, in the minds of the Czechs, a very special people. The news from America was always sensational. Sometimes we called it "Kachna," which meant something impossible or improbable. As I recall the news from our paper there existed an organization, whose members knew how to swear in different languages. Their president was able to swear in various languages for two days uninterrupted.

Our American heroes right after the War were United States Ambassadors, first Steinhard and after him Shirley Temple Black.

Ambassador Steinhard offered my friend Dr. Vaclav Wagner, employment at the Metropolitan Museum in New York. He was a great expert and he told me himself, "I could not accept it, because they would fire me in two weeks. I would tell them their paintings are copies, because we have the originals here in Europe."

Ambassador Steinhard helped my other friend, Dr. Ladislav Pinkas. He gave him a cottage in the United States to live. Nowadays, about 25 thousand Americans live permanently in Prague. It was very convenient for many to live very cheaply, some for $100 per month.

They have now English newspapers and a number of them teach English, which became, very fast, the second language.

I met my first American in the year 1935. I was a student in the sixth class of Archdiocesan Gymnasium. The studies, which were hard, did not ever bother me. My father, as was customary in those days, came to ask about my progress in studies. He was very disappointed and told me that in clear words, because the principal had told him, "Mr. Marek, I will tell you how it is with your son. His interests are first the music, second sports and the third school."

We had about 250 students, called "internists," in eight classes, who lived in a boarding school, run by the Jesuit Fathers and Brothers. We lived in 3 divisions, constantly watched by a prefect, who was a Jesuit, but not a priest yet. Above them was a "general prefect," who was a priest, not Czech, but a German, whom we admired very much, because he used to be the best goalie in Soccer in Austria, when he was young.

When he was young, the story goes, he liked a young lady. The song by Schubert evidently reminded him of her. It was the famous "Leise Flehen Meine Lieder" "Tise Ikaji Moje Pisne." ("My Song Flows Very Gently") It is a song full of Welt-Schmerz," as it used to be in those days.

34

In the Fifth and Sixth class of Gymnasium, three of us had a trio, Ota Cer-Mak on piano, Trubka Frantisek on trumpet and I on violin. We played at the silent movies and different other occasions. We practiced sometimes from 5 to 6 in the afternoon. That was strictly time for studying. General prefect caught us sometime and said, "You were supposed to be studying." I answered that we were studying this piece for a program. I had music by Schubert always on the pul-pit. He always mellowed and said, "Play it for me." We did!

I was not a bad student, but I wanted to be involved in competitions and races. On Saturday, I had decided to join the Invitational in the stadium "Slavia" in Prague. I sneaked out and worried constantly. In the Slavia stadium I won the 60 meters. Immediately, I was introduced to the new national coach, who was American Olympian, James Meredith. He wanted me to train with him, but I could not do it. He was the first American I saw.

The second American was Mr. Sullivan, who was in charge of American Catholic Charities in Prague after the war. About one million refugees were cared for by this organization. I tried to help and collected from the farmers of the parish. I administered a big truck of potatoes and shipped them to Prague.

Mr. Sullivan promised my friends that after my escape, he will help me if I came to Germany. The Communists did not want American Catholic Charities and proclaimed him persona not grata. He went to Frankfurt, where there was a big office for the whole of Germany. The top man was Father Bernard from Chicago and Pater Schneider from Milwaukee. The third one in charge of finances was Mr. Sullivan.

He was brave, because he took with him across the border his Czech secretary, who spoke English, Mrs. Stuchlilkova.

Chapter 15

I in Prague

I, Walter Marek, was born in Prague and that fact meant a special distinction, because there is a saying in the Czech republic, that if you were born in Prague, that "You were baptized by the river Moldau, in Czech "Vltava." The river Vltava flows through Prague and joins the river Elbe which is a mighty river, flowing from Bohemia North to the sea in Hamburg, Germany. River Elbe "Labe" is navigable from Pardubice, the city in East Bohemia, all the way to Hamburg and therefore is a very important transportation root in Central Europe. I was baptized shortly after my birth, mainly because of the effort of a nurse in the hospital. She was a German and she became my Godmother at the Baptism, where I also got the German first name, "Walter." It was an unfortunate choice, because in school I was ridiculed and constantly teased. I changed my name to "Vladimir" and a nickname "Lada," by which I am known even today in my former home town Horni Jeleni. I returned to Prague, when I was 11, when I was accepted in the Arch-diocesan Gymnasium which was considered the best school of that type in the whole Czechoslovakia. When I came back home for the first time for vacation, I was enthused, full of ideas and of missionary zeal.

Our class was especially strong in the Catholic faith and woe to everyone, who was making fun of it. We retaliated swiftly. For instance, one young lay professor of the Czech language, whom we admired, said something derogatory about our daily paper, published by our Popular Party, which was the Catholic and headed by a priest Msgr. Thdr. Sramek. He was our political leader, when Czechoslovakia was established in 1918. He was a member of the Parliament. The first thing Socialists wanted was to allow divorce. Monsignor Sramek fought that with his entire mind, so when he and his colleagues were thrown out of the assembly, they crawled back through the window. Prague was a very important place for me. As an individual it was important, but also as a member of the nation. Whenever I could, I went to see the culture and political events, of which some made an impression on me for the rest of my life. Even when I returned to Prague during and after the war it was always a very important time for me. In sports, I learned all that I wanted to know and in music my interest was to constantly grow. I went to Opera whenever I could and during the war I remember the people mistakenly waited in long lines until they realized that Mr. Lard (Sadlo) was the great Celloist playing that night.

Chapter 16

Czech Composers in Prague

Besides the famous Czech composers, internationally known, Dvorak, and Smetana, there are some modern composers from Prague. One of them, Rudolph Friml, came to America and became quite well known here. Rudoph Frimml, as a young man, lived in Prague where he dated a young lady. He was handicapped too. He had a harelip and the young lady ended up marrying his brother. Frimml composed about ten songs dedicated to her and then he left the country forever.

Another Czech, Karel Hasler, asked if he would mind if he gave his son fifty dollars and left him in New York and went to Hollywood. There he became a well known composer of music for films. His "Donkey Serenade" and his operetta "Rosemary" became well known. He always remained Czech and after the war he attended some meetings of the refugees in New York from where I know him. He was a shy man and married twice here. His second wife was his Chinese secretary. I was surprised once to hear his voice over the radio where he ridiculed and laughed at the music of Stravinsky. They evidently lived next to each other and I remember him speaking quite badly about his neighbor and especially about his music. Stravinsky became a most celebrated composer of modern times and his composition, "Right of Spring" is forever a great composition. Once it was first performed in Paris the impression was so deep and so controversial there was a riot in Paris because it was new music from a completely unknown.

Today, Prague has many composers. Some are able to come to the United States, like Vaclav Nelhybel. He attended the same school as I did in Prague and after maturity examination (like graduation) he didn't go to the priesthood, but he studied Greek and Latin languages in Prague. When the Germans arrested all the university students of Prague because they were demonstrating against their presence there, he was not taken because he ran to the conservancy of music and he was already known as a little composer at age 18. Thus, he was not taken like the thousands of other students to Orienburg concentration camp. He, eventually, came to the United States and here we met and for 25 years came to Blue Lake camp to conduct his pieces with the students there. He died suddenly in Pennsylvania.

Chapter 17

May 1, 1937 in Prague

In 1937, Europe lived in fear. We knew about the danger from Germany, but not much about the danger from Russia. On the 1st of May that year there was a very important demonstration by the Communist part of Czechoslovakia. They were going to show their might and power by demonstrating in Prague. It was well anticipated and I wanted to know personally about it. Therefore, I went in the morning about 10 o'clock to a place where the demonstration would go on the street, but I observed all of the precautions, never to smile towards the people who march, so I just looked. The police watched the procession as well, but weren't going to do anything because it would have caused a great riot in Prague.

First, came the band that played marches and then a procession of children and young people, then thousands of young woman wearing red scarves. It was a frightening sight. They shouted slogans, "Give us bread and work and you will not need the police." One younger woman came beside me where a police man was standing. She put her fist to his chin and didn't say much, but we all looked in horror wondering what would happen. The policeman didn't do anything and she proceeded on to march. Everyone wondered what would happen if these people eventually became in charge of our country.

They sang an international song which said, "If we march in millions we will reach our goals." and "Where is the power of our enemies." We lived in danger those days and we were targeted by propaganda.

First propaganda from Germany. I was told by a student that we are not a nation to be free and the consequences of it. On the other hand, from Russia, we had constant lures about the life of Communism. Once I met, during the war, a man who was an agent of Communism during the war. I was driving my bike on the highway, where we met and started talking. His main theme was, "Young man, remember the wind is coming from the east." That is what he told me when the Germans were on top of their power. He repeated it to me before we parted, "Remember young man the wind is coming from the east." The Germans knowing our feelings about their propaganda kept it constant during the war. They printed placards (like billboards), on which was the head of the man which was supposed to be Russian, but was a Mongol. His face was not clear. They said to us Czech's, "Is this your brother?" They knew that we Czech's thought of Russians as our Slavic brothers and hoped for liberation. These placards were everywhere. Later on there was another one posted of a Czech man named Joseph Smutek.

The Germans tried to catch him because he supposedly killed a German police man and escaped to England. After the war he came back and he became a member of our political party. I met him when he was about thirty years old (and I as well) at the time and I tried to use his abilities. He was a pilot in England when our political leader, Sramek, after a futile attempt to escape, sent Smutek and my secretary to investigate another possible rescue.

Chapter 18

The Irish in Prague

The Irish Nation has a similar history to our Czech nation. We are both small and suffered from domination of big neighbors. In Ireland, however, the persecution was very great. The Catholic priests were killed unless they escaped. Many escaped into Bohemia and Prague because after 1620 our country was very peaceful and welcomed refugees both from the east and from the west. One Irish man named Tafee became Supreme Judge of Bohemia and many others like Jesuits started Gymnasium and other school. They also liked the devotion to the Holy Infant of Prague which spread to Ireland and from Ireland to the United States. Many of them escaped to Bohemia and to Prague. One of them later even became the Judge of the Supreme Court of Bohemia. A group of Jesuits escaped and started a boys school, like the one which I attended.

Chapter 19

The Russians in Prague

The Russians came to Prague at the end of the war in 1945. I saw many big Czech Tatra cars taking Russian Generals to a banquet at the castle. Not only the military came to Prague, but some individuals also made it to Prague. They were mainly Jewish Russians who spoke some Czech quite easily and they became the governing part of Czechoslovakia. Naturally, the Czech Communists didn't like this and a great rivalry developed right at the beginning of Communism in 1948. Some Russians came with other Czechs from Russia. There were about 50,000 Czechs living in Russia and they were given permission to come back to their own country. I spoke once in Germany to a couple who were in it. They started from Russia on a train, thousands of them. When they came to the Polish boarding, they wouldn't let them go through. She said to me, "Suddenly a man jumped out from the train and talked to the Polish people and after some lengthy discussion they were able to continue on." The man's name was Wash. The same Mr. Wash became in Czechoslovakia the deputy of the Secret Police. He contacted our political party and offered some cooperation and interest. I was asked by our chairman what I thought of it, if he should continue the Shenanigans. I said to him please continue carefully and ask him for some vouchers for gasoline because he told me he saw in his purse all kinds of vouchers for food, gas and everything. I had plenty of gas now that he had given them to me. In two years, the Czech Communists had enough of this and accused the Czech Jews of treason and prosecuted them and hung them. Their leader Slanky was hung and I think Mr. Wash was among them as well. After that the Czech Communists continued their way and made everybody miserable. So, in 1968 some of them got fed up and wanted Communism with a human face, which is impossible. Their leader was Dubcek. Russia sent a big army of tanks to Prague to reverse the situation. Soldiers were told that there was a revolution there and had to conquer it, but the soldiers saw that it wasn't so and instead that we were peaceful some even knowing Russian and spoke their language. About 20,000 soldiers revolted and refused to fight. They were all captured and killed, and instead their families were told that they fought the Czech uprising.

Today, the presence of Russians is still strong in Prague. They have the Embassy which has hundreds of people. Many of them are spies or members of the secret police. They do not give up easy. I remember Russians who stayed in Litomysl after the war. Once I walked and met a Russian officer with whom I had a conversation. He told me, "Look at these villas here, it is unjust that some have a lot and some have so little." I said, "Do you have a son?" He replied, "Yes." I said, "You're telling me, that your sons and Stalin's sons have the same?"

He couldn't answer me. Stalin had two sons, one was captured by the Germans and we don't know his fate. It is said he refused cooperation. The other son was active after the way in hockey. He had a free hand from his father to make Russia a hockey power. He first ordered our national Czech team to go to Russia and play with the Russian boys until they developed the same skills. Then he bought movies about teams in the United States so they could learn about the teams and become the biggest and best team in the world.

When I was in school in 1936 we were hoping to win the Prague competition in volleyball. We got to the finals and faced the Russian team from the Russian Gymnasium in Prague. They were all refugees and bigger boys that us. Some of them were of Mongol nationality. We lost our pride and we learned to accept defeat.

Chapter 20

Popes in Prague

The last two popes visited Prague, Pope John Paul II and Pope Benedict XVI. It was a very great feast for the Czech Catholics. They number only 5% of the population now. They are very faithful and loyal to the Church of Prague. They exercise their political views in the Popular Party which was always very influential in the political scene of the Czech Republic.

The leaders were two priests, one of whom was Msgr. Joseph Sramcek, whose life was completely connected to the life of the church in Czechoslovakia. He was the leader of the Popular Party in 1918 when Czechoslovkia was just established after the collapse of Austria-Hungary.

There was a great movement against the Catholic Church led by three priests who were the leaders of the anti-movement. At the time more than a thousand priests petitioned the Holy See to be married and to have the Czech language in the Mass. They were rejected by the Vatican, Pope Benedict XVI, and they established a national church call Husistes. More than two million plus Catholics joined their church as well as many priests. So our nation was divided but the Catholics remained faithful, although they suffered a lot.

Into this situation one pope came to Czechoslovakia and his presence was a new vigor in the church. Pope John Paul II had no difficulty to speak our language, Czech. We admire the present pope, Benedict XVI, who is German. He also spoke Czech on certain occasions.

Msg. Sramek escaped to England before our country was occupied by Hitler. He became very important in our government, ...a prime minister. In that function he accompanied President Benesh to Moscow to thank Stalin for the liberation of our country. Stalin couldn't help but see the Catholic priests in charge of the new republic. He immediately suggested to Benesh to change the prime minister and he gave our country a man call Gottwald. Gottwald was a known communist. Sramek accepted his defeat and when the communists took power in 1948 he tried to escape again. This time it was the French government who helped and sent a plane to get Sramek and the other priests. However, Msgr. Sramek was caught.

Chapter 21

St. Agnes of Bohemia

There are three St. Agnes': St. Agnes of Rome, St. Agnes of Hungary, and St. Agnes of Bohemia. It is St. Agnes of Bohemia with whom we are concerned. In Czech she is called Anezka. She was born in 1205 in Prague, now the Czech Republic.

St. Agnes of Bohemia wanted to enter the convent to be a nun. However, for political reasons, she was promised in marriage. She was eventually promised to the Holy Roman Emperor, Frederick II. Pope Gregory IX intervened into this arrangement and procured a release for Agnes acknowledging she was already betrothed to the "king of heaven".

Agnes entered the convent of the Poor Clare nuns of St. Saviour in Prague with the aid of five nuns sent by St. Clare of Assisi. She was professed on Pentecost Sunday in the year 1234 and ultimately became the abbess of the convent. Agnes spent 50 years in the cloister.

She was more than generous with her wealth , especially with the poor. Agnes built a Franciscan Hospital and developed the staff to minister its related clinics. She would often cook for the other sisters and mend clothes for the lepers.

Agnes had the gifts of healing and prophecy and remained close to St. Clare of Assisi through correspon-
dence.

Agnes of Bohemia is a shining example of Christian faith
and heroic charity. She remains a model of courage and
spiritual help for young people who consecrate themselves to the religious life. Her feast day is March 2.

Epilogue

"My Bed on Fire?"

As in my previous book, I would like to conclude this one on a light note.

I sleep in a hospital bed. When I received it, our friend, who is a master electrician, told me this bed was not properly wired. He told me the bed could catch on fire because of this. Therefore, I didn't plug it in. However, when the painters came to paint my room, they were very good people, very efficient and conscientious. After their job, they put my bed back to the wall, and noticed the cord with a plug. They plugged it in. But, they didn't tell anybody about it. For several days, nothing happened, but one morning, I woke up when the mattress started on its own to fold up. It folded with me in it. It was a very funny feeling for me. It stopped only when both ends of the mattress almost touched each other above me. I felt like a pretzel inside. I tried to wiggle and maneuver a little bit, but the mattress did not move at all. Luckily, I got out and left the bed. When I found out the bed was plugged in, I unplugged it, but the mattress had her own mind. It unfolded by itself automatically. I use the bed in peace now that it is kept unplugged.

This is my second book after the age of Ninety. Certainly, I remember so many things which I could write about, but I selected those which might be meaningful to all of you who visit Prague and are interested in Czech history. I am thankful to all of you who helped me to write this book and I would like to bring a few dreams yet to reality. There is so much to be done in music for young people and there is so much to be learned about our life which I know is so precious.

Thank you and God bless America.